AL'S HAM-'N'-EGGER
&
BODY SHOP AGAIN

by

PETER WHITSON WARREN

The Basilisk Press
Fredonia, N.Y. 1974

ACKNOWLEDGMENTS

Some of these poems were previously published in the following magazines and are reprinted here with the editor's permission: *A Nosegay In Black*, *Nimrod*, *Riverside Quarterly*.

Cover Photo of Whitson and Mat at the Mexican Gulch Western Dakota Stage Station by Dick Wheeler.

ISBN 0-913560-07-3

CONTENTS

IV 3 LEGENDS

V SUSAN

FOR SUSAN
& FOR LESLIE

AFTERNOON, MEMORIAL DAY, NORTH LIBERTY, IOWA, 1966

The small tom cat
runs by the kitchen door
with a large mouse,
stops to see
if he is followed.

Your eyes are green.

I have sent myself a letter
to pass time
and watch
a farmer's wife
harrow with a big green tractor,
while her husband,
in another field,
plants corn.

You are memorizing German
aloud, gather sunlight
with your hands.

In Viet Nam young girls
are burning themselves.
And the 500 has 12
cars left.

My hands smell of grass.

4 FOR LESLIE ON THE 25TH OF APRIL

1
My head hurts
from last night's beer
from being alone too long
from being beaten with a new amaryllis
and a jonquil.

2
In the distance
old tanks move across snow
naked soldiers walk on the water
the sky is black
no wind.

3
Above me
floating
a photograph of Anouk Aimee
as large as China.

4
There are words in the sky
and you are smiling
light touching your glasses
light refracted to 1000 colors.

A LESLIE IN A CEMETERY

'I went, supposedly, to draw
but, really, to sit and dream,
empty headed, in the sun.'

A softness.
Strange, quiet happiness.
Your legs are crossed,
your skirt wrinkled and orange,
the grass damp.
Sun, touching your face,
has taken the fear of being engulfed by earth,
of throwing up your own stone.
Syringa are budding,
and the stones reach out forever.
Their whiteness,
so like new snow
in quiet mountains.
Your not unhappiness
has reached all the way to Montana.

3 DAYDREAMS

NO. 12

Wind through holes
in the crumbling logger's shack
and rain
falling on my belly .
Walls are bare–
the old Life magazines used for reading.
In the morning I will find you
on a yellow horse
running toward white topped mountains.

NO. 4

Blond children run in the tall grass
of small farms in New Hampshire.
The air is clean.
In the dark parts of forests
pink lady slippers have blossomed.
And all the wars have ended.

NO. 763

In Kennebunk, Maine
there is a house
                    in the sea.
Its boards are black
         or gray (dark)
                 We have just awakened
                             beneath a blanket
of foam.

EPITAPH

Whitson '71

IN IOWA

for James Wright

Gray cats
fretfully nurse their litters
in cold barns.
Pregnant hogs scrape the frozen mud
and grunt at their weight.
It is March.

There will be green in the fields soon:
I am a visitor used to mountains
and wait for corn
to block out neighboring farms.

I hear the big green tractors
all day and men with hammers
mending fence.
I am growing quiet
and old here
and watch for sea gulls.

ON THE FARM IN NORTH LIBERTY,

the sun is lower,
cold.
The tomato plants are dead.
We light fires in the evening,
& the cats come in.

I think of graves
& apples,
while Arthur,
fat cat on the floor,
Thinks of milk.

People rioting in Cincinnati.

Sidney & Sybelle are out,
looking for mice
beneath the brooder house.
The chickens died last summer,
some disease.

My friends are killing
& dying
in Viet Nam.

& the kittens,
5,
are in their box,
wanting to get out,
to explore the house.

Earlier,
from the television,
the explanation of our search
for life on Mars.

LOOKING FOR SUN

1
The plastic of a patched-up window
rattles drops of last night's rain
onto the sill.
Water stands in the dark fields
where corn is up.
It is cold for June.
And, thinking of gardens,
I light the mud brown stove,
watch a meadow lark
fly over the brooder house
looking for sun.

2.
Above me,
in a drawing,
a fat bellied Indian Chief
grins as he injects novocain
into his face.
A purple iris has blossomed
in a glass of water
beside my hand.

AND NOW,

because the leaves fall
from their branches,
the mountains come out,
brown and blue,
to make the horizon.

EPITAPH

> *'Our other event in London—*
> *a trip to Westminster Abbey*
> *and who should be buried there,*
> *in a choice spot, but you.'*
> Norman Klein

1
Sir Peter Warren,
'Knight of the Bath,
Vice Admiral of the Red Squadron
of the British Fleet
and Member of Parliament
for the City and Liberty of Westminster,'
who had long hair
and was shorter
than my shortness,
has lain, some years,
beneath the marble bust
of himself.
But then, if I am he . . .

2
Sprinklers water the lawns of ugly houses
        in Billings, Montana.
And fat children waddle over the cracked streets.

The big ugly Plymouth sits,
        without tail or brake lights,
          in the corner of my crushed rock yard.
Bugs have eaten the nasturtiums and hollyhock.

A glittering pink next door bicycle
on my step.

3
Small blonde children, laughing, mow the next door lawn—
scissors and an old push mower sounding a recalcitrant rhythm.

The garbage cans by my house are full of a stink.
And the birds are gone—black and purple birds

that were here yesterday, on my roof, the branches of my tree.
Pregnant cats, chasing, ate them in their minds.

Tree needles turning brown. Some wax on a floor.

4
All our lives have come together,
become something.
Full of a fear,
and we are all going.
We hope our nasturtiums will not die.

As new shoes,
we have become beautiful,
white and black
black and white.

And now,
on the moth breath of a falling star,
an old man lifts his cane
and points to some red roses
that are dying.

THE BILLINGS POEM

1
A light snow
has covered the lawns and sheets of Billings, Montana.
Brown fog solidifies,
toward tomorrow,
on the branches of trees.
On the South Side
an old Indian, crying, "I am not dead!"
is beaten unconscious by police,
left in the snow of a forgotten alley.

2
I try to sell the photographs I no longer want,
pieces of the women I've loved.
The powder of bones.
An old man is calling for his grave
and his dog.
Every morning
I awake, take pills, medicine
and dream of Algonquins.

3
Where are the children and the gray cats
that sleep in trees beside the birds?
Where are the old men who spoke so eloquently
of love?
I cannot find a name
in the frozen branches of the moon.
I have come this far
and found myself alone.

BILLINGS CEMETERY/JIMMY JOE–DOUBLE IMAGE

Side by side wooden markers:
Fred Loeffler   1860-1913
Bernice Loeffler   1863-1910.

In Red Lodge, Jimmy Joe Ayling
moves nervously through his cabin
getting books he's packed, "I'll go back
home soon. In May." (another cabin
toward Cooke City), blue prints of whalers,
"I always double 'em."

Rotten concrete. White stones of the war dead in rows:
George Giles   G.A.R.
Fred Loomis   Civil War.

He's small, white hair
shining in the light from his just washed windows,
his New Jersey accent sounding strange
in Montana's Absarokas. He's seen
Hong Kong and London many years ago.
"Hitler lost the war 'cause he's only a corporal
not a general like Von Hindenburg and Bismark."

Homer W. Summers:
Died Aug. 23, 1892, aged 14 yrs. 2 ds–
"Peaceful be thy slumber,
Peaceful in thy grave so low.
Thou no more will join our number,
Thou no more our sorrows know."

"You've got your freedom, Kid,
don't let 'em take it away–

Commies, Niggers, Jews, One Worlders
(the U.N., National Council of Churches).
You gotta go underground,
you gotta kill 'em, Kid!"

Charles H. Getchell died at 88,
outlived his wife and daughter,
lies beside them and a budding bush.

He will not give his age,
just says he's been around.

Broken marble
and the great concrete tree trunks.
Eathan Rickman has a white
picket fence around his small plot,
black letters on his wooden stone
and plastic flowers.

Thursdays he goes to town,
Chommie, his white husky, pulling the wagon,
his beard blowing, tourists stopping
to photograph.

Minnie Carlson died in 1922.
A bush grows from above her head,
plastic flowers above her belly,
a white wood marker with blue letters,
around her a low white peeling wood wall.

THE LOST LADY & OTHERS

Whitson '71
3-35697

A ROSE FOR MARTHA

1
Light streaks through cloud holes
halo farms near Springfield, Missouri.

2
I am above the clouds (tree clouds,
mountain clouds with faces
of the Presidents, cotton candy clouds,
mushroom clouds),
returning
with rain streaks across my window,
the horizon rusted to something,
my face empty,
my foot sore from jeweled ceilings
and a kindly old prince
who wanted my mind blanked.

3
It will be 78 degrees in Cedar Rapids.

SOME NEW TIMES AND OLD PLACES

for Joan

1
Last night, shutting the old Plymouth's vent window,
I crunched my hand right through it.
Flakes of glass in snow.

2
My face has a growth of hair
all over. Even the eye-ball sockets.
Fine soot and tom cats are coloring
the snow and a wing-flapping stock-car-bird.
Icicles are not dripping.

3
A month ago, I put you on a train.
Off to Iowa City,
some new riots and a dog named Michael.

4
I had a week of loving you.

5
Now.
You are in Jacksonville, where there is no snow.
And I am making a rug
of pieces from a garbage can.

DAYDREAM NO. 137

for Joan

Above me,
on a crab apple branch,
a crow is talking:
"Cowboys once owned
this land."
I am not a cowboy.

If I were,
I'd ride a black horse
to your door.

THE FLOWERS OF SPRING

for Cena

The sky yellows to evening,
and new foot prints pass the dark house.
Abandoned now,
the tulips and crocuses I gave you last fall
are green spears beneath a mid-April snow.
There is so little time anymore
and so much.

IN MONTANA

for Cena

'I have come a long way
to get this far.'

1
Beneath me
the soft gumbo
slides, imperceptibly, toward darkness.
Melting late April snow
covers grass, already green.
It is spring again.

2
In the old gray hotel
strong silent women
nervously pace abandoned rooms.
Car noise fills the night-gray sky
with echoes of a summer of happiness.
And the Bucket-of-Blood Bar crashes
into itself
(with no one to hear).

3
Many Montana men, long dead,
slide with the gumbo.

POEM WRITTEN AFTER ARRIVING HOME OCTOBER 24, 1970 AND FINDING NO LETTER FROM "THE LOST LADY"

1
The few yellow leaves still on their branches
are bright birds in January snow.
And the silence is a watch with no hands.

I have come home to this
after climbing a hill I thought was a mountain,
the way back.

2
In Springfield, you feed chickens, chop wood,
ask the Watchman to be yourself
or your self to fly, silent, bird-like,
over that mountain, the way back.
The way back to what?

Nancy, we both fear,
hide in our respective houses (mine the smaller),
drink beer or wine, make pictures of the sky inside
our skulls. That silent sky
we don't really want but think we should.

3
A week ago, in the alley, by my front door,
I found a pair of knitted red mittens,
put them, brightly, on the fence
for the little Nancy or Peter who lost them.

They are still there.

3 LEGENDS

THE LEGEND OF FROSTOP PAM or THE ONLY OFFICIAL & TRUE STORY OF FROSTOP PAM (NO. 2)

Frostop Pam acquired her name by working at the Frostop Drive In on Broadwater Ave. in Billings, Montana for 2 weeks in August of 1970 & before Frostop Pam was Frostop Pam she sold hot dogs on sticks at the Midland Empire Fair in Billings & before that she strung beads at the Western Dakota Junk Co. (also in Billings) & before that she just sort of hung around the Junk Co. & looked for a job & before that she was in New Hampshire.

& at the Frostop Drive In (or Carhop) Frostop Pam served hamburgs & root beer & fish sandwiches to teeny boppers & old people & she wore brown corduroy pants or Levis & an old sweat shirt & tennis shoes or hiking boots & sleepy green eyes & a rubber band around her long blonde hair & everyone thought she was a bit nuts (& she was or is) & she read Dylan Thomas in a corner when there were no customers & the other Frostop Carhop girls would ask her if it was a good book & she didn't know what to say because that was such a dumb question.

& Frostop Pam would get a ride to work at the Frostop Carhop at 7:00 in the morning in a beat-up old 1937 Plymouth & at 4:50 in the afternoon or a little before the beat-up old 1937 Plymouth would be back & the funny old bearded man who drove it would order a hamburg & some milk & Frostop Pam would bring them to him & he'd eat & drink them & then at 5:00 Frostop Pam would get into the beat-up old 1937 Plymouth & sometimes the funny old bearded man wasn't finished eating his hamburg & drinking his milk & Frostop Pam would have to sit there in the beat-up old 1937 Plymouth while he finished them & all the other Frostop Carhop girls walked back & forth in front of the car pretending that they weren't staring & then they'd all

(Frostop Pam & the funny old bearded man & the beat-up old 1937 Plymouth but not the other Frostop Carhop girls) go back to the Junk Co. where they lived with a lot of other people & they'd do things like drink beer & talk & make-up stories all night long (which is why Frostop Pam wore sleepy green eyes).

& this went on day after day & then Frostop Pam quit working at the Frostop Carhop & the day after Frostop Pam quit working at the Frostop Carhop she went to the mountains with a bearded fellow named Mat (a different bearded fellow than the funny old bearded man with the beat-up old 1937 Plymouth) & spent 2 days going up hills (& mountains) & down hills (& mountains) & trying to catch fish & other dumb stuff.

& then they went back to the Junk Co. & the next day (August 27th to be exact) Frostop Pam & all the other people who lived at the Junk Co. (except the funny old bearded man with the beat-up old 1937 Plymouth who had always lived there & the other bearded fellow named Mat who didn't really live at the Junk Co. but just hung around there a lot) got into a black 1963 Oldsmobile with air conditioning & power windows & a power seat & a lot of other stuff & went back to New Hampshire where they live with a lot of other people at Poison Ivy Acres in Barrington.

& on September 7th they all got on the phone (a difficult feat) & said happy birthday to the funny old bearded man with the beat-up old 1937 Plymouth who is still at the Western Dakota Junk Co. in Billings (because he owns it) where he lives alone with a fat gray cat named Sybelle.

& that same funny old bearded man with the beat-up old 1937 Plymouth has told me to tell you that he loves Frostop Pam (but then everybody loves Frostop Pam).

EPILOG:

& on September 12th Frostop Pam & all the other people at Poison Ivy Acres sent the funny old bearded man with the beat-up old 1937 Plymouth a Rubber Duckie on wheels & the Rubber Duckie on wheels was painted with daisies & "SLUJ" & Frostop & peace symbols & psychedelic stuff & the funny old bearded man with the beat-up old 1937 Plymouth dearly loves his Rubber Duckie & he pulls it along behind him everywhere he goes (but he doesn't go to the Frostop Carhop anymore).

THE LEGEND OF THE LOST LADY
&
THE LOST LADY MINE

The Lost Lady rode into Billings, Montana on the Western Dakota Stage on September 27, 1894 (I think it was a Sunday) & she'd come from Oregon in record time (28 days) & only 1 hold-up & only one Indian attack (in Mexican Gulch) both of which were thwarted by 3 Finger Jack who was riding shotgun on the Western Dakota Stage & was famous for thwarting hold-ups & Indian attacks & actually had 8 fingers & 2 thumbs & I don't know why he was called 3 Finger Jack except that he had this thing about being called 3 Finger Jack & he was a pretty good shot & the Lost Lady had come to Billings to visit with friends & her face was sad.

& on the first night the Lost Lady was in Billings she met a funny old bearded man who'd just rode into town on an old gray mule named Baa & she met him because he came over to the house she was staying at & they all (the Lost Lady & the funny old bearded man with the old gray Mule named Baa & the people the Lost Lady was staying with) sat around all night long drinking beer & swapping lies & the Lost Lady didn't say much & mostly drank beer & listened (she was tired from the trip & the Western Dakota Stage wasn't exactly a Pullman) & then the funny old bearded man with the old gray mule named Baa went home on his old gray mule named Baa & he didn't see them & they didn't see him until Wednesday when they went to the funny old bearded man with the old gray mule named Baa's house (a little sod hut on the alley of what was to be 76 years later the busiest street in Montana) where they drank a lot more beer & swapped a lot more lies & the Lost Lady talked more this time after she looked at a lot of books the funny old bearded man with the old gray mule named Baa's book case (they say he was some sort of school teacher) & the funny old bearded man with the old gray mule named Baa invited them to go with him to Gramma's Saloon on Friday night.

& Friday night they all (the Lost Lady & the funny old bearded man with the old gray mule named Baa & the people the Lost Lady was staying with) went to Gramma's Saloon in the buckboard that belonged to the people the Lost Lady was staying with (the funny old bearded man with the old gray mule named Baa's old gray mule named Baa was night blind or they'd have gone in his beat-up old 1837 manure wagon) & the Lost Lady & the funny old bearded man with the old gray mule named Baa danced all night long until almost 2 a.m. & the Lost Lady was happy & had a happy face & smiled all night long & they drank beer all night long (the people the Lost Lady was staying with danced a few dances & drank a lot of beer too) & the Lost Lady & the funny old bearded man with the old gray mule named Baa very drunkenly staggered back to the house where the Lost Lady was staying with her friends (the friends the Lost Lady was staying with had gone home much earlier as they were tired & drunk & sort of old but not as old as the funny old bearded man with the old gray mule named Baa) & the Lost Lady & the funny old bearded man with the old gray mule named Baa talked all the way home & held hands & had their arms around each other & stuff like that & the funny old bearded man with the old gray mule named Baa kissed the Lost Lady good night (it was a long kiss & about 30 minutes) at the door of the house where the Lost Lady was staying & then the funny old bearded man with the old gray mule named Baa went home to his sod hut on the alley of the street that was to be 76 years later the busiest street in Montana & dreamed Lost Lady dreams all night long.

& on the very next day (Saturday to be exact) the funny old bearded man with the old gray mule named Baa & the people the Lost Lady was staying with took the Lost Lady to the Western Dakota Stage Station in the buckboard that belonged to the people the Lost Lady was staying with (the Lost Lady & the funny old bearded man with the old gray mule named Baa had to ride in the back with their feet over the edge as they had the night before when they went to Gramma's Saloon & danced all night long until almost 2 a.m. & the Lost Lady was happy & had a happy face & smiled all night long & they drank beer all night long but I've said all that before) & they (the funny old bearded man with the old gray mule named Baa & the people the Lost Lady was staying with) put the Lost Lady on the noon Western Dakota Stage to Oregon & when the Lost Lady got back to Oregon after 28 days & 1 more hold-up & 1 more Indian attack both of which were thwarted by the great & famous 3 Finger Jack she got a job in the Lost Lady Saloon in Springfield & became the belle of the town.

EPILOG:

& many years later (76 to be exact) a funny bearded fellow named Mat (a different bearded fellow than the funny old bearded man with the old gray mule named Baa) was walking on some range land in Mexican Gulch, Montana & found an old abandoned coal mine & on a badly worn & weather-beaten sign by the entrance to this old abandoned coal mine was "THE LOST LADY MINE" & whatever the hell that has to do with the Lost Lady or the funny old bearded man with the old gray mule named Baa or the people the Lost Lady stayed with in Billings, Montana in 1894 I haven't the vaguest idea.

Whitson '71

AL'S HAM-'N'-EGGER & BODY SHOP

Al's Ham-'n'-Egger & Body Shop used to be in Baa, Western Dakota but it burned down 1 Thursday afternoon in May of 1937 & it was a nice fire & all the children in the town brought wieners & roasted them & afterwards they roasted marshmallows in the coals & Baa, Western Dakota didn't have a fire department or a fire truck or even a fire extinguisher so the children didn't have to worry about getting wet.

But before Al's Ham-'n'-Egger & Body Shop burned down 1 Thursday afternoon in May of 1937 it was a thriving business serving ham & eggs & bacon & juice & fixing bodies all at the same time & on the same stove & all this was done by Al who was about 30 & bald & wishing he had a wife to take over the body shop part because he was a better cook than a body fixer & he didn't really like bodies or understand them but the only unmarried woman in Baa, Western Dakota over 12 was almost 94 & didn't like Al or bodies.

& after Al's Ham-'n'-Egger & Body Shop burned down 1 Thursday afternoon in May of 1937 Al took his insurance money (Al's Ham-'n'-Egger & Body Shop was insured for a lot more than it was worth when it burned down 1 Thursday afternoon in May of 1937 & a lot of people & especially Al's insurance agent wondered about that for a long time) & went to Clark Street in Chicago & became a wino which is what Al had always wanted to be anyway & you can find Al & talk to him about Al's Ham-'n'Egger & Body Shop but you have to check all the doorways on Clark Street because Al never sleeps in the same doorway twice in a row & Al's older now & balder & sometimes he can't talk too well because he's usually drunk or passed-out & he hasn't used up all the insurance money from when Al's Ham-'n'-Egger & Body Shop burned down 1 Thursday afternoon in May of 1937 yet.

SUSAN

AL'S HAM-'N'-EGGER & BODY SHOP AGAIN

for Susan of Fried Egg Fame

Quiet morning,
too cold for old Plymouths.
Instant breakfast.

In 1963 I wrapped a 50 Plymouth
around a giant oak tree.
That finished it.
2 days in shock.
Yeah, drunk.

A yellow-brown '70 Camaro stops at
Al's Ham-'n'-Egger & Body Shop,
and you get out,
go in,
order bacon and eggs
over light,
while the left rear dent
is pounded out,
filled,
disappears
until
next time.

AL'S HAM-'N'-EGGER
& BODY SHOP

PLUGGING THE PLYMOUTH IN
or THE DAYS BEFORE CHRISTMAS

1

A few dry swirls on the packed snow,
boots squeak.
You are home in Miles City,
a place I've never been.
I plug the Plymouth in,
take milk and Gelusil
for the pain in my duodenum .

2

The amaryllis bud bends from the light,
toward the stove.
Icicles, hanging across the gray window,
drip and drop into the shallow snow.
I plug the Plymouth in,
take milk and Gelusil
for the pain in my duodenum.

3

The apaloosa and the palomino colt,
thinking with their bellies,
come for a hand full of long hay.
They have been pawing the drifted snow
after the summer's grass
and continue when the hay is gone.
At home,
the Plymouth is plugged in from yesterday.
I take milk and Gelusil
for the pain in my duodenum.

4

The bright sun, shining the snow, looks warm,
is not.
You are home in Miles City,
a place I've never been.
I plug the Plymouth in,
take milk and Gelusil
for the pain in my duodenum.

PIECES

Walking on the 32nd St. snow,
walking in the 10 below cold
of another January morning,
steam rises from the cars
and mouths (a pink coated girl
walking, parallel, across the street).

Yesterday's 4 o'clock knock on your door
brought no answer,
so I left a card
signed, Al,
and danced away, running, down 22nd St.,
sliding corners in the old Plymouth.

I dreamed you last night
or this morning,
forgot the dream,
as the cold slipped in,
and the morning's sunless light
began a day with no shadows.

Now, later, and the light has gone,
12 below, and I'm writing you these words,
pieces of my skull
that fall, prearranged, on the paper,
pieces I must hammer down
nail to the snow on my feet.

ANGELA, MONTANA AND THE SEARCH FOR SPRING, FEBRUARY 7, 1971

1
We lift the frozen bales to the high green truck,
your father and I,
while the tight gray cat crouches in their shadow,
hiding from the cold wind,
crying for spring
and a warm rain.

You are warm
inside the cab, engine running,
warm inside my head,
my looking for spring
and a green New Hampshire field.

2
Yesterday
we had our worst fight,
all silence,
running away to the narrow little alleys
of safe loneliness.

We came back, though,
back to the uncertainty of giving of ourselves,
back to the good loneliness of being one together
at sunrise
or early afternoon
of a new spring thaw.

3

You drive the truck,
a slow idle through the cattle,
horses, the 1 ewe,
your father breaking bales
at their feet.

Free from the cold,
I sit,
warming, beside you,
can already see the green
and the bank high stream.

THE WESTERN DAKOTA JUNK CO.–
THE FIRST POEM

Wrapped in your rose covered comforter,
your head 4 high on the slipless pillows,
you turn, quietly screaming
at the sadness of your dreams,
as the slow freight by the junk yard
rumbles this couple-small house
and the clouded stars.

Soon, the cab will come
(a Yellow Cab with a thick junk dealer
sunk beneath the cracked wheel)
to take me past the neoned shops and gas stations,
take me to the Western Dakota Junk Co.,
my house, with its 1 yellow outside bulb
all night long.

I watch your dreams,
that sadness beneath your lidded tight eyes,
wishing I could crawl inside,
crunch all the bent faced men and grinners,
as the junk yard press does a gray '47 Plymouth,
and just curl up there,
being your pink smile.

THE WESTERN DAKOTA JUNK CO.–THE FOURTH POEM

There are new leaves.
It is Spring again.
And I have looked for you
Everywhere.
–Albert Simmons

A robin sings from that ancient Chevy cowl
in the weeds by my front door.
And the cold comes in,
sliding off the rims and hills,
silent, invisible,
and as personal as earth.

I am alone,
I am getting fat
from too much beer,
squat on the blood red carpet,
an old Algonquin on a 1 way street
making-up dreams
for a future that is past.

The rain has stopped,
3 days of rain that made mud
for that new red carpet
and kept the Junker, the old gray Plymouth,
missing,
stalling,
and the grass greener.

I have been alone so long
        I don't know what it is to be free.
(They'll wonder,
        in the bars,
                where I am).
But I have a light
        that shines on a white clothesline post
                and the green weeds
                        and that Chevy cowl.

A POEM FOR SUSAN, WRITTEN ON MAY 2, 1971 AT 115½ GRAND AVENUE, BILLINGS, MONTANA

1
Sybelle, the fat gray cat,
sits in the bathroom window
looking out,
watching,
as the day goes dark
and the yellow leaves go green.

2
The sound of power mowers
slips under the door,
as I make paintings of Montana,
brown and green
with a white sky
and a dotted line
to heaven.

3
Hello Susan,
I hope you are happy
and free as you wish.
There are tulips
and amaryllis
about to bloom.

Whitson '71

BY NOW THE FACE IS GONE

1

By now the face is gone
        missing
& the daylight so full of battered toys
        the legless doll baby
        the run-over black car
        the lead soldier
                not alone
                not left

I mail you pieces of myself
                daily

The gray soldiers arrive
        & the Marines
your-left-your-left-your-left-right-left
        ghost like
        floating
                across the dented daylight
                a sadness
        to be alone
        to be

& children
        delicate as dust
        searching
                for fathers
                mothers
                for sisters
for their own faces

finding
instead
the lead soldier
& no finger holds

By now the face is gone

2
Entering the plain white tomb
& finding dishes unwashed
made a bright amaryllis
white
rushing over November snow
small darkened leaves on the green carpet

3
By now the face is gone
missing
so much water over Buttermilk Falls
the Taughannock
that far away

& thick pictures of mountains
floating across the yellow moon

In New Hampshire
the mountains are small
& there are no abandoned mines
there was nothing to mine
so long ago
1500 miles or so
away

4

I've taken to wearing a gun
        Confederate 44
                made in Paris
accurate as spitting
powerful as a lead soldier
        foolishness
                drying on the faces

I am in Montana's Absarokas
        stalking a dream
                lost
                        alone lost

        So far away

Are you coming

5

By now the face is gone
        missing
& the candle's thin smoke
slips across the sun
        coming up
                again
                again

The stuff of golden rings
the stuff of tomorrow
        missing
        again
& the sky brightens
leaving a lead soldier
        in the wings

& a child
& the black car

A young girl
walking in a park
        made of sadness

An old man
asking for his cat
        his cane
                & tomorrow

By now the face is gone

& I NEVER KNOW IF THEY'RE REAL

Sometimes
when I'm alone
        enough
        & it's been raining
                enough
                (spring rain)
        I see things I've never seen before
paper bags that float in under the old Plymouth
old men with stainless steel walkers
        to pull themselves about
new Camaros with small dents in their fenders
        (always groups of 3)
& I never know if they're real

THE MONUMENT

For Susan

"The monument to Sir Peter Warren,
Knight of the Bath, which can be seen
even today in Westminster Abbey,
was erected, shortly after his death
in 1752, by his wife Suzanne."
Albert Simmons

1
The burned-out Skyline
atop the Rims
has black leaning walls,
has sky through vacant windows,
has time
lost.

It had 3 floors,
28 rooms,
then
thick black smoke
that kept big jets from landing,
that roofed the West End like a sky.

2
The bright cars pass slowly,
people come just to look,
to watch the thin light smoke
still rising,
take home
an isolated keepsake.

3

Remember,
Susan,
when we came up for fondue,
for beers,
for painting back-lighted images of the past
on concrete walls.

I've lost
that time,
I can no longer even dream you here,
I can no longer see your face,
the 2 miles and 3 months we've been apart
are not your distance.

4

The burned-out Skyline
atop the Rims
has black leaning walls,
has sky through vacant windows,
has time
lost.

Six hundred copies have been printed offset by Service Print at Dunkirk, New York, of which two hundred are numbered and signed by the author.